RONALDO

The Complete Story of a Football Superstar

100+ Interesting Trivia Questions, Interactive Activities, and Random, Shocking Fun Facts Every "CR7" Fan Needs to Know

HOUSE OF BALLERS

YOUR FREE BONUS!

>> SCAN THE QR CODE BELOW TO GAIN EXCLUSIVE ACCESS <<

Contents

Introduction 5

Chapter 1: Birth & Childhood 7

Chapter 2: Foray Into Football & Youth Career 15

Chapter 3: Emergence At Sporting Lisbon And Transfer
To Manchester United 23

Chapter 4: Becoming A Man At Manchester United 31

Chapter 5: The Spanish Dream 40

Chapter 6: Mr Champions League 49

Chapter 7: The Italian Affair 57

Chapter 8: Manchester Re-United 66

Chapter 9: International Career 75

Chapter 10: Profile And Style Of Play 85

Chapter 11: Individual Accolades And Personal Records 93

Chapter 12: Personal Life & Philanthropy 101

INTRODUCTION

The name "Cristiano Ronaldo" is not only instantly recognizable as that of a true modern great, it is perhaps the most famous name on planet Earth. One only needs to take a look at the series of unbroken feats and laudable achievements that its owner has recorded to understand why.

Cristiano Ronaldo was born in the Island of Madeira to a poor Catholic family, but he managed to outshine the circumstances of his birth to become one of the most recognized faces in the world and has built a legacy that will never be erased.

From impressing Sir Alex Ferguson by single handedly dismantling a far superior Manchester United defense in his days at Sporting Lisbon, to his unstoppable heroics against Atletico Madrid, and constantly keeping Portugal among the big boys, Cristiano Ronaldo has always surpassed expectations and imaginations.

The story of his rivalry with Lionel Messi for two decades will never be replicated ever again. His signature moves will forever evoke emotions from the watching audience. Everywhere he has played, from Old Trafford to the Bernabeu, from Allianz Arena to Camp Nou, fans have been left astonished by his wand of a right leg, his bullet of a left leg, and his aerial prowess has downed many great sides. He has all the accolades and trophies he needs to prove that he is the G.O.A.T.

But how did Cristiano Ronaldo make the journey from a gangly teenager with freckles, into the chiseled record-breaker notable for his good looks, philanthropy, and amazing footballing ability? How did he make the trip from promising prospect to record goalscorer in three top leagues? How did he become Mr. Champions League? How did he become the most followed human being across social media?

Ronaldo

In this Ronaldo trivia book, we take a look at his life, career and record-setting exploits. Laid out in twelve chapters, we take a quick look at the highlights of arguably the greatest man to ever kick the football. He has seen it all – amazing goals, incredible clutch moments, hattricks, titles by the bucketload, fiery moments, record leaps, stunning transfers, legal tussles, and insane commercials. This book tells the tale of Cristiano.

Very few people have had as storied a career as Cristiano Ronaldo, and here's your chance to catch up with the most important moments in his career!

Are you a Ronaldo fan? Do you want to know more about your idol? Are you trying to know more about his playing style? Do you want to know why he has no tattoos? Are you intrigued about his relationship with Sir Alex Ferguson?

Then, you are holding the right book in your hands.

Lean back and learn about Cristiano Ronaldo, the boy who became the man that conquered Europe for Portugal in a few pages!

CHAPTER

1

BIRTH & CHILDHOOD

"We've had some great players at this club in my 20 years, but he's up with the best."

- Sir Alex Ferguson

Ronaldo

10 Trivia Questions

1. Ronaldo's paternal great-grandmother was from the island of _____?

    A. Madeira

    B. Cape Verde

    C. Comoros

    D. Barbados

2. How many siblings does Ronaldo have?

    A. 2

    B. 4

    C. 3

    D. 1

3. Ronaldo was brought up in a parish called_____?

    A. Sao Pedro

    B. San Mames

    C. San Jose

    D. Santo Antonio

4. At what age was Ronaldo diagnosed with a heart condition?

    A. 15

    B. 13

    C. 12

    D. 11

5. What is the name of Ronaldo's only brother?

 A. Hugo

 B. Nuno

 C. Jorge

 D. Joao

6. In what month was Ronaldo born?

 A. January

 B. February

 C. March

 D. April

7. Ronaldo was added to Cristiano's name after as a tribute to_____?

 A. Ronald Perelman

 B. Ronald Koeman

 C. Ronald Reagan

 D. Ronald Colman

8. Ronaldo was born in the year_____?

 A. 1990

 B. 1982

 C. 1980

 D. 1985

9. Ronaldo's father had a job in football as a_____?

 A. Coach

 B. Groundman

 C. Kitman

 D. Journalist

10. For which offense was Ronaldo expelled from school?

    A. Starting a fire

    B. Killing a pet

    C. Starting a fight

    D. Throwing a chair at a teacher

10 Trivia Answers

1. B – Cape Verde

2. C – 3

3. D – Santo Antonio

4. A – 14

5. A – Hugo

6. B – February

7. C – Ronald Reagan

8. D – 1985

9. C – Kitman

10. D – Throwing a chair at a teacher

Cristiano Ronaldo dos Santos Aviero was born on 5 February 1985 in the Sao Pedro parish of Funchal, capital of the Portuguese island of Madeira. He was the last of four children born to Maria Dolores dos Santos Viveiros da Aveiro, a cook, and José Dinis Aveiro, a municipal gardener and a part-time kitman at local club Andorinha.

Ronaldo's paternal great-grandmother, Isabel de Piedade, was of African descent, from the island of Cape Verde. Ronaldo has an elder brother, Hugo, and two elder sisters, Elma, and Liliana Cátia "Katia". Ronaldo was brought up in a poor Catholic Christian home in Funchal's Santo Antonio parish, where he shared a single room with his siblings.

In fact, Ronaldo's mother intended to abort him as she believed she already had enough children and was worried about the family's poverty and his father's alcoholism. However, her doctor turned down her request for the procedure.

Ronaldo was added to Cristiano's name as a form of a tribute to Ronald Reagan, his father's favourite movie star and the United States president at the time. Ronaldo was enrolled at Escola Basica e Secudaria Goncalves Zarco, but he did not complete school beyond the sixth grade as he agreed with his mother to quit school and play football semi-professionally at the age of 14. Despite his popularity with other kids at school, he was expelled for throwing a chair at a teacher after what he perceived as disrespect from the teacher. At the age of 15, Ronaldo was diagnosed with Tachycardia, a heart condition that could have jeopardized his football career, but he underwent laser surgery to correct the defect.

CROSSWORD #1

ACROSS

(2) Birth month

(5) Most played team

(7) Team after Portugal

(9) Balon D'Or wins

(10) #1 sport in England

DOWN

(1) CR7's nationality

(3) Birth city

(4) First team

(6) Name in the USA

(8) First trophy for potugal

FORAY INTO FOOTBALL & YOUTH CAREER

"He has magic in his boots. The first thing you notice about him is that he is incredibly quick and very, very powerful for such a young man."

- *Eusebio*

10 Trivia Questions

1. At which of these clubs did Ronaldo start to play football?

   A. Nacional

   B. Maritimo

   C. Sporting

   D. Andorinha

2. Ronaldo joined Sporting's youth academy after a trial that lasted how many days?

   A. 10

   B. 20

   C. 3

   D. 5

3. How many appearances did Ronaldo make for Sporting B?

   A. 40

   B. 2

   C. 20

   D. 10

4. Which of these clubs did Ronaldo move to in 1995 at the age of 10?

   A. Nacional

   B. Maritimo

   C. Sporting

   D. Andorinha

17

5. How much did Sporting pay to sign Ronaldo to their youth academy?

    A.   100 pounds

    B.   1500 pounds

    C.   20,000 pounds

    D.   500 pounds

6. Ronaldo left school at what level to focus on football?

    A.   Fifth grade

    B.   Seventh grade

    C.   Sixth grade

    D.   Fourth grade

7. How many goals did Ronaldo score for Sporting B?

    A.   0

    B.   10

    C.   20

    D.   1

8. Ronaldo's first official game for Andorinha was against_____?

    A.   Nacional

    B.   Maritimo

    C.   Sporting

    D.   Camara Lobos

9. How many official games did Ronaldo play for Andorinha?

    A.   10

    B.   200

    C.   52

    D.   35

10. How many goals did Ronaldo score for Andorinha?

    A. 10

    B. 20

    C. 15

    D. 8

10 Trivia Answers

1. D – Andorinha

2. C – 3

3. B – 2

4. A – Nacional

5. B – 1500 pounds

6. C – Sixth grade

7. A – 0

8. D – Camara Lobos

9. C – 52

10. D – 8

As a result of his father's association with local club Andorinha, where he worked as a kitman, Ronaldo had a childhood steeped in football. He played for Andorinha from 1992 to 1995 and he received his first individual accolade on August 1st, 1993 in the Adelino Rodrigues children's tournament where he was named Best Player.

The 1993/94 season was his first official season for Andorinha and he scored a goal in the team's first official game against Camara Lobos while donning a number 7 jersey. After 8 goals in 52 official games for Andorinha, Ronaldo moved to Club Deportivo de Nacional, known commonly as Nacional in exchange for 20 footballs and a set of football kit for kids.

After a three-day trial with Sporting Club de Portugal in 1997, Ronaldo was signed on to the club's youth ranks for 1,500 pounds. That meant that he had to move from Madeira to Alcochete, near Lisbon. He endured a brief spell on the sidelines due to heart condition that needed surgery in 2000, before a spree of successive promotions saw him reach Sporting's first team in the 2002/03 season. He made only two appearances for Sporting B and was not fortunate enough to get on the scoresheet either.

Ronaldo

EMERGENCE AT SPORTING LISBON AND TRANSFER TO MANCHESTER UNITED

"The kid makes you sick. He looks the part, he walks the part, he is the part. He's six-foot something, fit as a flea, good-looking - he's got to have something wrong with him."

- Ian Holloway

10 Trivia Questions

1. Ronaldo was promoted to Sporting's first team in which of these seasons?

    A. 2001/02

    B. 2002/03

    C. 2004/05

    D. 2006/07

2. Who was Sporting's first team manager at the time of Ronaldo's promotion to the first team?

    A. Jose Mourinho

    B. Fernando Santos

    C. Laszlo Bastoni

    D. Johann Cruyff

3. Ronaldo made his Sporting debut against which of these teams?

    A. Braga

    B. Vitoria Setubal

    C. Moreirense

    D. Porto

4. What was Ronaldo's jersey number in his lone season with Sporting's first team?

    A. 7

    B. 13

    C. 15

    D. 28

5. How many league goals did Ronaldo score for Sporting in the 2002/03 season?

    A. 3

    B. 5

    C. 8

    D. 10

6. What was the fee involved in Ronaldo's transfer to Manchester United from Sporting?

    A. 25 million pounds

    B. 12 million pounds

    C. 5 million pounds

    D. 8 million pounds

7. Ronaldo's first goal for Sporting was scored against _____?

    A. Maritimo

    B. Moreirense

    C. Braga

    D. Porto

8. How many appearances did Ronaldo make for Sporting's senior team?

    A. 31

    B. 20

    C. 15

    D. 10

9. How many Portuguese players had been signed by Manchester United before Ronaldo?

    A. 3

    B. 2

    C. 1

    D. 0

10. Ronaldo made his Manchester United debut against_____?

    A. Leeds United

    B. Bolton Wanderers

    C. Charlton Athletic

    D. Everton

10 Trivia Answers

1. B – 2002/03

2. C – Laszlo Bastoni

3. A – Braga

4. D – 28

5. A – 3

6. B – 12 million pounds

7. B – Moreirense

8. A – 31

9. D – 0

10. B – Bolton Wanderers

During the 2002/03 season, Cristiano Ronaldo was promoted to Sporting's first team after his pace and dribbling abilities caught the eye of the club's first team manager at the time, Laszlo Bastoni. He became the first Sporting player to feature for the Under-16, Under-17, Under-18, reserve, and first team in a single season when he was handed his first team debut on September 29th, 2002 in Sporting's 4-2 loss at Braga in the Portuguese Primeira Liga.

He scored a brace in a 3-0 win over Moreirense just over a week later. He scored 8 goals in 25 appearances for Sporting that season. His representatives suggested him to Barcelona president, Joan Laporta, then Liverpool manager, Gerard Houllier, and also held a meeting with, then Arsenal manager, Arsene Wenger, over a potential move.

But it was legendary Manchester United manager, Sir Alex Ferguson, that sanctioned a move for the talented teenager after watching him up close in United's 3-1 reverse to Sporting in an August 2003 friendly that marked the opening of Sporting's Jose Alvalade Stadium.

Ferguson described Ronaldo as "one of the most exciting young players" he had ever seen as United parted with 12.24 million pounds, the highest fee ever paid for a teenager in English football at the time to make Ronaldo their first ever Portuguese recruit. And what a recruit he turned out to be!

The transfer was completed on August 12th, 2003 and Ronaldo was handed the number 7 jersey worn by iconic former United players such as George Best, Eric Cantona, and David Beckham instead of the number 28 he requested and used to wear at Sporting. Ronaldo made his Manchester United debut on August 16th, 2003, during a 4-0 Premier League win over Bolton Wanderers, coming on as a second half substitute for Nicky Butt.

Word Scramble #1

Unscramble these words to solve the puzzle!

1. NAICSTOIR ROAOLND _____

2. SSNHPIA AL GLIA _____

3. OATG _____

4. HTE BETS _____

5. FIAF LRDWO PCU _____

6. ITLAINA IEERS A _____

7. LTPRUOAG _____

8. MNHOCSPAI GLEUAE _____

9. AGLENDN ERMPEIRE LEGEUA _____

10. OUREENPA PAONIHHPCMIS _____

11. TCNHRSAEEM UDIETN _____

12. EARL DRIMDA _____

13. TNEUSVUJ _____

14. TPO REOCSR _____

15. NAPSI _____

16. CRKTTHAI _____

17. DLENGO OBTO _____

18. OLANB RDO _____

19. EKRISRT _____

20. CLGAOO _____

BECOMING A MAN AT MANCHESTER UNITED

"There have been a few players described as the new George Best over the years, but this is the first time it's been a compliment to me."

- George Best

Ronaldo

10 Trivia Questions

1. Ronaldo's first Premier League goal was scored against which of these teams?

   A. Watford

   B. Middlesbrough

   C. Portsmouth

   D. Everton

2. How many games did Ronaldo play for United in his first season at the club?

   A. 20

   B. 40

   C. 25

   D. 10

3. Who were the opponents when Ronaldo scored his first hattrick for United?

   A. Millwall

   B. Portsmouth

   C. Tottenham

   D. Newcastle United

4. Ronaldo received his first red card against which of these teams?

   A. Aston Villa

   B. Blackburn

   C. Chelsea

   D. Derby

5.   Ronaldo scored United's 1000th Premier League goal against which team?

    A.   West Brom

    B.   Middlesbrough

    C.   Southampton

    D.   Fulham

6.   How many trophies did Ronaldo win in his second season at United?

    A.   3

    B.   2

    C.   1

    D.   0

7.   Ronaldo was banned by UEFA in the 2005/06 season for what offense?

    A.   Kicking a ball boy

    B.   Destroying a corner flag

    C.   Inappropriate gesture

    D.   Dissent

8.   How many goals did Ronaldo score for United in the 2006/07 season?

    A.   23

    B.   15

    C.   17

    D.   55

9.   Ronaldo captained United for the first time in a home win against which team?

    A.   Liverpool

    B.   Bolton Wanderers

    C.   Reading

    D.   Wigan

10. Ronaldo scored his 100th Manchester United goal against which team?

    A. Everton

    B. Fulham

    C. Sunderland

    D. Stoke City

10 Trivia Answers

1. C – Portsmouth

2. B – 40

3. D – Newcastle United

4. A – Aston Villa

5. B – Middlesbrough

6. D – 0

7. C – Inappropriate gesture

8. A – 23

9. B – Bolton Wanderers

10. D – Stoke City

Cristiano Ronaldo received a standing ovation and performed admirably well on his debut that George Best described it as "undoubtedly the most exciting debut he had ever seen." Ronaldo's first goal for United was scored from a freekick in a 3-0 Premier League win over Portsmouth on November 1st 2003. He scored three more Premier League goals in the second half of that season, the last of which came against Aston Villa in the final league game of the season, in which he also got sent off. He finished his first season at United by scoring the opening goal of United's 3-0 win over Millwall in the 2004 FA Cup final, earning the first major trophy of his career.

Ronaldo scored United's 1000th Premier League goal in a 4-1 defeat at Middlesbrough at the end of October 2004 and produced memorable displays in wins against Aston Villa and Arsenal at the start of 2005. United returned to the 2005 FA Cup final as holders but lost 5-4 on penalties to Arsenal although Ronaldo converted his spot kick during the shootout.

Ronaldo endured a tumultuous third season at United as he clashed with teammate Ruud van Nistelrooy who took offense at the Portuguese's flamboyant style of play. Ronaldo also incurred a one-match ban from UEFA due to a middle-finger gesture at Benfica fans during a UEFA Champions League game, and got sent off in the United's 3-1 defeat in the Manchester derby for kicking ex-Manchester United striker, Andy Cole. Ronaldo put all of those frustrations aside to help United to success in the 2006 League Cup, scoring the third goal in a 4-0 final victory over Wigan Athletic.

Ronaldo was rumored to have asked to leave Manchester United in the summer of 2006 after a bust-up that saw teammate Wayne Rooney sent-off in Portugal's victory over England at the 2006 World Cup. Ronaldo's request was turned down and he got booed throughout the 2006/07 season although his 23 goals in all competitions helped United to a first Premier League title in four years and the semifinal of the UEFA Champions League where United lost to AC Milan and the FA Cup final where United lost to Chelsea after extra time.

Ronaldo set a new club record for most United goals in a single season, as his 42 strikes in 2007/08 helped United to a Premier League and UEFA Champions League double.

Ankle surgery kept Ronaldo sidelined for the first couple of months in the 2008/09 season but he returned to help United to the 2009 League Cup and also edge out fierce rivals Liverpool in a nervy Premier League title race to claim a third successive championship crown.

Ronaldo also helped United reach a second straight UEFA Champions League final, memorably scoring a FIFA Puskas award-winning 40-yard screamer at Porto in the second leg quarterfinal, and a brace in the second leg semifinal win at Arsenal. Ronaldo scored the last goal of his first stint at United from a freekick in a 2-0 Manchester derby win at Old Trafford.

WORD SEARCH #1

```
P  S  L  E  N  H  N  Y  W  L  X  I  S  Q  K
O  R  X  A  X  X  T  L  O  E  L  R  E  B  Q
R  V  L  U  I  P  C  I  R  R  C  K  R  S  Y
T  S  G  F  J  S  H  I  L  O  X  V  I  A  K
U  E  N  G  L  A  N  D  D  N  C  G  E  X  P
G  N  C  E  H  Y  B  F  C  A  H  O  A  T  M
A  D  A  B  H  Q  Z  Z  U  L  A  A  Q  H  B
L  P  B  H  E  H  F  A  P  D  M  T  B  E  A
K  E  U  R  O  S  I  Z  L  O  P  I  R  B  L
M  Y  I  U  N  K  F  B  V  W  I  K  G  E  L
M  W  Y  R  U  D  A  L  A  A  O  M  U  S  O
Y  L  A  L  I  G  A  O  H  R  N  J  X  T  N
X  V  U  G  F  V  W  O  C  P  S  C  W  S  D
S  K  Z  E  W  W  F  X  N  K  W  Y  U  Y  O
A  W  V  Q  D  I  A  L  A  Q  V  O  T  H  R
```

RONALDO	THEBEST	SERIEA	ENGLAND
LALIGA	WORLDCUP	PORTUGAL	BALLONDOR
GOAT	FIFA	CHAMPIONS	EUROS

CHAPTER

5

THE SPANISH DREAM

"Cristiano is unique for his talent and professionalism – he is also extraordinarily consistent… [He] is an outstanding professional. He's committed to the team and the club, he doesn't talk much, but he is a leader."

- Carlo Ancelotti

10 Trivia Questions

1. How much did Real Madrid pay to acquire the services of Ronaldo?

    A. 70m pounds

    B. 90m pounds

    C. 80m pounds

    D. 85m pounds

2. What was Ronaldo's jersey number in his first season at Real Madrid?

    A. 7

    B. 9

    C. 11

    D. 17

3. How many goals were scored by Ronaldo in his first season at Real Madrid?

    A. 33

    B. 31

    C. 29

    D. 26

4. Ronaldo's first competitive appearance at Real Madrid was against which team?

    A. Barcelona

    B. Athletic Bilbao

    C. Sevilla

    D. Deportivo La Coruna

5. Ronaldo's first Champions League goal at Real Madrid was scored against which team?

   A. Lyon

   B. FC Zurich

   C. Marseille

   D. AC Milan

6. Ronaldo scored a first La Liga hat trick for Real Madrid against which team?

   A. RCD Mallorca

   B. Real Betis

   C. Valencia

   D. Villareal

7. Which was Ronaldo's most prolific season at Real Madrid?

   A. 2010/11 season

   B. 2012/13 season

   C. 2014/15 season

   D. 2016/17 season

8. In what year was Ronaldo's last goal in *El Clasico* scored?

   A. 2014

   B. 2019

   C. 2020

   D. 2018

9. Ronaldo scored five times in a match for the first time against which team?

   A. Almeria

   B. Granada

   C. Sevilla

   D. Malaga

10. Ronaldo played his last league game for Real Madrid against which team?

    A. Villareal

    B. Valencia

    C. Celta Vigo

    D. Leganes

10 Trivia Answers

1. C – 80m pounds

2. B – 9

3. A – 33

4. D – Deportivo La Coruna

5. B – FC Zurich

6. A – RCD Mallorca

7. C – 2014/15 season

8. D – 2018

9. B – Granada

10. A – Villareal

After coming very close to pinching Cristiano Ronaldo away from Manchester United in the summer of 2008 as a direct replacement for Brazilian winger Robinho who had joined United's closest rivals, Manchester City, Real Madrid finally completed the signature of Ronaldo for a then world record fee of 80m pounds in the summer of 2009.

The Portuguese winger arrived amidst exuberant fanfare in the Spanish capital, as Real Madrid's Santiago Bernabeu Stadium was sold out for his unveiling ceremony. He was handed the number 9 jersey by legendary former Real forward, Alfredo Di Stefano, as his favored number 7 was unavailable at the time and held by Madrid legend, Raul.

Ronaldo scored in his first four league games to become the first Real player to achieve the feat, and ended his first season as the club's highest goalscorer with 33 goals. Ahead of the start of his second season at Real, Ronaldo picked up the number 7 jersey which was now available following the departure of Raul Gonzalez, and led Real Madrid to their first trophy in 3 seasons, memorably heading in an extra time winner against fierce rivals Barcelona in the 2010/11 Copa del Rey final.

Ronaldo scored 60 goals in all competitions to help Real Madrid set a La Liga record of 100 points and claim a first championship in four years, as well as reach the UEFA Champions League semi final for the second successive season. Ronaldo claimed his third piece of silverware at Real by helping the capital-based side to the Supercopa de Espana at the start of the 2012/13 season, edging out Barcelona on away goals rule following a 4-4 aggregate score. Ronaldo scored 55 goals in as many games as Real finished runners-up in the La Liga and Copa del Rey and reached a third successive UEFA Champions League semifinal in the 2012/13 season.

The arrivals of Italian manager Carlo Ancelotti and Welsh winger Gareth Bale (with whom Ronaldo and Benzema formed a formidable attacking triumvirate dubbed as "BBC", an acronym for Bale, Benzema and Cristiano) helped Real Madrid capture the 2014 Copa del Rey and an elusive tenth European crown in the 2013/14 season, with Ronaldo netting a competition record 17 strikes as he won a second UEFA Champions League title.

Despite collecting no silverware with Real Madrid at the end of the 2014/15 season, Ronaldo set a new personal best record of 61 goals for the season, as his 48 league goals earned him a second successive *Pichichi* (La Liga top goalscorer) award and third overall, and his ten goals in the UEFA Champions League meant he has finished as the competition's top scorer for a third successive season.

Ronaldo became Real Madrid's all-time top goalscorer during a topsy-turvy 2015/16 campaign for Real Madrid that finished with the club capturing a second UEFA Champions League title in three seasons. In the 2016/17 season, Ronaldo's 42 strikes in all competitions helped Real to a La Liga and UEFA Champions League double, at the same time making Real the first club to win successive European crowns in the UEFA Champions League era. The 2017/18 season turned out to be Ronaldo's last in Spain as he scored 15 goals in the UEFA Champions League to finish as the competition's top scorer for an outrageous sixth straight season (and seventh overall) and help Real clinch a third successive European crown in his final game with the club.

CROSSWORD #2

ACROSS

(2) 3 goals

(4) Spanish Cup

(5) Position after 30

(8) Portugal team color

(9) Nickname

(10) Team in Italy

DOWN

(1) 5 Trophies

(3) Top scorer trophy

(6) Position before 30

(7) English Cup

MR CHAMPIONS LEAGUE

"Ronaldo has come through for the past two or three years, and is the best in Europe. I think at the moment no doubt Ronaldo is the best player."

- Pele

Ronaldo

10 Trivia Questions

1. Ronaldo's first ever UEFA Champions League goal was scored against_____?

   A. Roma

   B. Lyon

   C. Fenerbahçe

   D. Celtic

2. How many games did it take Ronaldo to score his first Champions League goal?

   A. 2

   B. 27

   C. 14

   D. 32

3. How many Champions League hattricks were scored by Ronaldo at Manchester United?

   A. 3

   B. 2

   C. 1

   D. 0

4. Ronaldo has played in how many UEFA Champions League semifinals?

    A.   9

    B.   10

    C.   21

    D.   12

5. How many players other than Ronaldo have scored in three Champions League finals?

    A.   0

    B.   1

    C.   2

    D.   6

6. Ronaldo broke the record for most Champions League goals in a single season in_____?

    A.   2014/15

    B.   2015/16

    C.   2016/17

    D.   2013/14

7. Ronaldo's first Champions League hattrick was scored against _____?

    A.   Galatasaray

    B.   Ajax

    C.   Schalke

    D.   Malmo

8. Ronaldo scored his 100th Champions League goal against which of these teams?

    A.   Juventus

    B.   Atletico Madrid

    C.   Bayern Munich

    D.   Tottenham Hotspur

9. Ronaldo's became the first player to reach 100 Champions League wins against_____?

    A. Valencia

    B. Lyon

    C. PSV

    D. Benfica

10. Ronaldo's last Champions League hattrick was scored against_____?

    A. Juventus

    B. Malmo

    C. Bayer Leverkusen

    D. Atletico Madrid

10 Trivia Answers

1. A – Roma

2. B – 27

3. D – 0

4. C – 21

5. A – 0

6. D – 2013/14

7. B – Ajax

8. C – Bayern Munich

9. A – Valencia

10. D – Atletico Madrid

Since the reformation of the old European Cup that gave birth to what is now known as the UEFA Champions League, no player has dominated it as much as the legendary Portuguese forward, Cristiano Ronaldo.

The former Manchester United, Real Madrid and Juventus star is the most prolific player in the history of the competition with 140 goals, and he is the only player in the competition's history to score in three different finals, doing so with Manchester United against Chelsea in 2008, and repeating the feat with Real Madrid in 2014 and 2017 against Atletico Madrid and Juventus, respectively. No player has won more titles than the five Ronaldo has won, and he has finished as top scorer an on an unrivalled seven occasions.

Ronaldo has made the most appearances in the UEFA Champions League (183), scored the most goals in the knockout stages (67), scored the joint most hattricks (8), won the most finals (5), scored the most goals in a single season (17), and is the only player to score in 11 consecutive matches.

Ronaldo was also the first to achieve double figures for goals in the UEFA Champions League group stage and one of only two players to score in all six group stage games. Ronaldo's 10 goals against former club Juventus is the most any player has scored against a particular opponent in the competition's history.

Ronaldo's remarkable UEFA Champions League scoring record seems all the more extraordinary when one notices that his first goals arrived in his 27th game in the competition, a brace in Manchester United's 7-1 rout of AS Roma in the 2006/07 UEFA Champions League quarterfinal second leg match.

The first of his 8 competition hattricks was scored while playing for Real Madrid in a 4-1 win at Ajax in October 2012. Ronaldo became the first player to score 100 UEFA Champions League goal in Real Madrid's 4-2 win over Bayern Munich in the 2016/17 quarterfinal second leg, clocked a century of wins in the competition in a win against Valencia in 2018, and scored his 140th goal in a 2-0 win for Manchester United at Villareal in November 2021.

Ronaldo

CHAPTER

7

THE ITALIAN AFFAIR

"It is impossible to replace Cristiano. It doesn't matter who you sign. He has left the club, and you can sign quality players, but they will not achieve what he did at this club, but that is football."

- Zinedine Zidane

10 Trivia Questions

1. When was Ronaldo's transfer to Juventus from Real Madrid completed?

    A. June 2017

    B. July 2018

    C. August 2019

    D. September 2018

2. Ronaldo made his Juventus debut in a Serie A game against _____?

    A. Sassuolo

    B. Hellas Verona

    C. Chievo Verona

    D. Sampdoria

3. Ronaldo scored his first goal for Juventus against which of these teams?

    A. Inter Milan

    B. Lazio

    C. Napoli

    D. Sassuolo

4. Ronaldo scored his 10th Serie A goal against _____?

    A. Fiorentina

    B. Bologna

    C. Cagliari

    D. Palermo

5. How many Serie A appearances did Ronaldo make during his time at Juventus?

    A. 150

    B. 98

    C. 50

    D. 75

6. Ronaldo won his first trophy at Juventus following a win against _____?

    A. Napoli

    B. Lazio

    C. AC Milan

    D. Fiorentina

7. How many trophies did Ronaldo win at Juventus?

    A. 0

    B. 3

    C. 2

    D. 5

8. How many league goals did Ronaldo score in his first season at Juventus?

    A. 19

    B. 12

    C. 30

    D. 32

9. Ronaldo's 100th Juventus goal was scored against which of these teams?

    A. Sampdoria

    B. Sassuolo

    C. Parma

    D. Torino

10. Ronaldo made his last appearance for Juventus against which of these teams?

    A. Empoli

    B. Spezia

    C. Udinese

    D. Atalanta

10 Trivia Answers

1. B – July 2018

2. C – Chievo Verona

3. D – Sassuolo

4. A – Fiorentina

5. B – 98

6. C – AC Milan

7. D – 5

8. A – 19

9. B – Sassuolo

10. C – Udinese

Following their 3-1 win over Liverpool in the final of the 2017/18 UEFA Champions League, Cristiano Ronaldo spoke of his time at Real Madrid in the past tense, fueling speculation of an imminent departure from the Madrid-based outfit.

His prosperous 9-year association with Real Madrid ended on 10 July 2018, when the 5-time Ballon d'Or winner transferred to Juventus in a move worth an initial 100 million euros, with a further 12 million euros in add-ons and solidarity contributions to his youth clubs.

The fee is the highest paid by an Italian club and also the highest for a player over 30 years old. Ronaldo cited his desire for a new challenge and lack of support from Real Madrid president Florentino Perez as some of the reasons for his exit from Madrid.

Ronaldo made his Juventus debut in a 3-2 Serie A win at Chievo Verona and scored his first two goals in a 2-1 Serie A home win over Sassuolo in what was his fourth appearance for the Turin-based outfit, with his second strike of that game bringing him up to 400 career league goals. He was sent off in his first UEFA Champions League game for Juventus against Valencia, but became the first player to win 100 matches in the same competition as he set up Mario Mandzukic's winner in the return leg against the Spanish side.

Ronaldo won his first piece of silverware with Juventus in January 2019, heading in the only goal of the game to down AC Milan in the 2018 Supercoppa Italiana. He matched Giuseppe Signori's single season record for most successive away league games with at least one goal when he scored in a 3-0 win at Sassuolo in February, and also scored a hattrick against Atletico Madrid in March to fire Juventus into the last 8 of the Champions League.

Ronaldo became the first player to win championships in England, Spain, and Italy in April 2019, as a 2-1 home win over Fiorentina clinched Juventus' eighth consecutive Serie A title. Ronaldo finished the season with 21 goals and 8 assists, and was named the inaugural winner of the Serie A's Most Valuable Player award.

Ronaldo scored 31 league goals in his second season at Juventus as the club made it 9 Serie A titles on the bounce. His 37 goals in all competitions earned him the club record for most goals scored in a single season.

In what turned out to be his third and final season in with Juventus, Ronaldo added a second Supercoppa Italiana and a first Coppa Italia to become the first player to win every domestic trophy in England, Spain, and Italy. His 29 league goals earned him the *Capocannonerie* (highest goalscorer) award, making him the first player to finish a league season as top goalscorer in England, Spain, and Italy.

Ronaldo started the 2021/22 season at Juventus, coming on as substitute in their 2-2 draw against Udinese, but left the club in the final week of that summer's transfer window.

WORD SEARCH #2

```
G T B O S Q S T C X X U O O D
A O X C M A N U N I T E D G B
S P J J M J U H A T T R I C K
U S Z R T U R D H K J R Q I W
G C L F Q V G E A C S Q S G X
O O N R I E Z R T D T L Q A Y
L R J E A N F B F H N T E K I
D E Y E A T N Y O Z B N K C T
E R L K Q U W P O A W F L C B
N S O I B S F B H E A D E R D
B I Y C R E A L M A D R I D C
O Z C K T S P A I N K O P K R
O O M Q T B Y V C B V E I Z D
T A J A T I X N I Y X T B H A
I A R H F F X V T H Q G N C G
```

MANUNITED	REALMADRID	FREEKICK	JUVENTUS
HEADER	TOPSCORER	SPAIN	HATTRICK
GOLDENBOOT	DERBY		

MANCHESTER RE-UNITED

*"Any great player would be welcomed back, but Cristiano
went beyond being just a great player. I'm a fan of him
like anyone else and on a personal level I would like to see
him back. I can't say anything more than that."*

- Sir Bobby Charlton

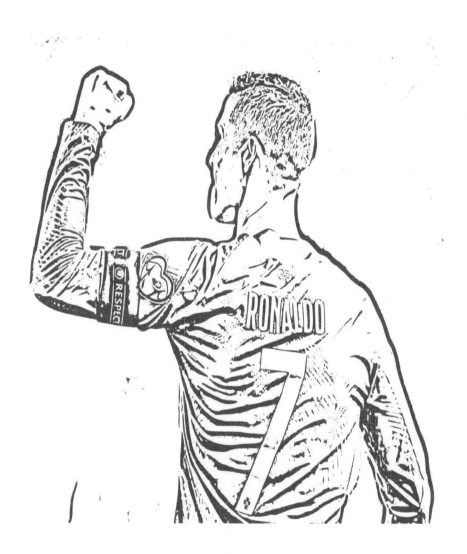

10 Trivia Questions

1. Ronaldo played his first game back at United against _____?

   A. Leeds United

   B. Southampton

   C. Wolves

   D. Newcastle United

2. How many hattricks did Ronaldo score in his first season back at United?

   A. 4

   B. 2

   C. 1

   D. 0

3. Ronaldo's first Champions League goal in his second stint at United was against_____?

   A. Young Boys

   B. Villareal

   C. Atalanta

   D. Atletico Madrid

4. How many Champions League goals did Ronaldo score in his second spell at United?

   A. 10

   B. 2

   C. 6

   D. 0

5. How many Manchester derby appearances did Ronaldo make in his second spell at United?

   A. 3

   B. 2

   C. 1

   D. 0

6. Ronaldo scored his 50th club hattrick against _____?

   A. Tottenham

   B. Norwich

   C. Arsenal

   D. Newcastle United

7. How many Premier League goals did Ronaldo score in his second spell with United?

   A. 19

   B. 20

   C. 21

   D. 22

8. Ronaldo's 700th career goal was scored against_____?

   A. Fulham

   B. Chelsea

   C. Everton

   D. Wolves

9. How many trophies did Ronaldo win in his second spell at United?

    A. 3

    B. 2

    C. 1

    D. 0

10. Ronaldo's final appearance of his second United spell was against_____?

    A. Sheriff

    B. Fulham

    C. Aston Villa

    D. Chelsea

10 Trivia Answers

1. D – Newcastle United

2. B – 2

3. A – Young Boys

4. C- 6

5. D – 0

6. B – Norwich

7. A – 19

8. C – Everton

9. D – 0

10. C – Aston Villa

Ronaldo

Manchester United agreed a deal with Juventus to re-sign former superstar player Cristiano Ronaldo five days after the Portuguese forward's last appearance for the Bianconeri. The move was worth an initial 12.85 million pounds, a little over what United paid to sign Ronaldo from Sporting Club of Portugal 19 years before.

The contract length was set at two years with the option of a third year, and Ronaldo was allowed to have the number 7 jersey as Edison Cavani, to whom the number 7 belonged at the time of the transfer had agreed to switch to number 21.

Ronaldo made his second debut for Manchester United in a Premier League game against Newcastle United at Old Trafford on 11 September, and scored a brace in a 4-1 win for the home side.

He became the first player to score in five successive UEFA Champions League games for an English club, as his six group stage goals helped United to emerge as group winners. Ronaldo was named Premier League Player of the Month in April 2022 and finished the season as the Premier League's third highest goalscorer with 18 goals. He also won United's Sir Matt Busby Player of the Year award, but missed out on club silverware of any kind for the first time in 12 years.

Amid growing frustration and dissatisfaction with United's fortunes on and off the pitch, Ronaldo missed United's pre-season tour of the Far East and speculation was rife that he sought a move to club competing in the UEFA Champions League, despite the insistence that he was part of the club's plans and was not available for a transfer by new United manager Erik Ten Hag. In any case, his age, overall cost of any potential transfer, and exorbitant wage demands scuppered any chance of a move.

Ronaldo featured sporadically, mostly as a substitute in the early stages of the campaign, getting most of his playing time in the Europa League. He scored his 700th career goal after coming on as a first half substitute for the injured Anthony Martial in a 2-1 win at Everton on 9 October, but refused to be subbed on and left the stadium before the end of a home win against Tottenham Hotspur 10 days later. Ronaldo was barred from first team training and dropped for the trip to Chelsea, but was allowed to rejoin the group after discussions with the manager.

Ronaldo scored the third goal in United's home win over Sheriff that secured passage to the next round of the Europa League, and was named captain for the trip to Aston Villa that ended up in a 3-1 defeat. He missed United's final game before the World Cup, before his interview with TV personality, Piers Morgan, that revealed the discord between Ronaldo and the management hierarchy at United was published on 14 November. United sought legal advice on possible breach of contract on Ronaldo's part before a mutual termination of his contract with immediate effect was agreed on 22 November 2022.

WORD SEARCH #3

```
S   I   V   I   U   Z   Z   K   Y   I   G   Z   M   Y   N
K   N   W   C   Y   U   T   J   T   C   L   J   G   Q   C
I   S   S   E   W   D   K   D   K   O   Z   H   L   X   S
L   P   S   L   H   W   F   A   C   N   J   U   Z   H   B
L   I   X   E   Q   L   E   A   D   E   R   S   H   I   P
S   R   V   B   S   U   P   Q   N   T   M   M   A   S   V
U   A   J   R   P   A   T   H   L   E   T   E   M   G   D
L   T   G   I   E   A   U   T   L   R   M   M   B   I   E
W   I   S   T   E   T   P   O   W   E   R   R   I   V   D
D   O   E   Y   D   H   S   R   S   G   Q   C   T   T   A
U   N   Y   U   O   H   B   C   B   T   Q   M   I   R   Y
O   S   T   R   I   K   E   R   J   D   B   B   O   L   E
C   C   X   G   D   H   N   R   Y   L   P   C   N   M   R
V   D   E   D   I   C   A   T   I   O   N   H   O   Q   D
B   P   E   E   P   L   A   Y   E   R   S   B   K   J   O
```

PLAYER	AMBITION	STRIKER	SKILLS
SPEED	CELEBRITY	ATHLETE	INSPIRATION
POWER	DEDICATION	LEADERSHIP	ICON

INTERNATIONAL CAREER

"He is the best. The best in the world, yes. Probably the best ever. I saw Maradona a couple of times. I never saw Pele. But Cristiano is amazing. This man is the best. Cristiano is a goal machine."

- Jose Mourinho

Ronaldo

10 Trivia Questions

1. How many caps did Ronaldo win across Portugal's youth levels?

    A. 0

    B. 34

    C. 11

    D. 22

2. Ronaldo came on as a substitute for which player on his senior Portugal debut?

    A. Rui Costa

    B. Pauleta

    C. Luis Figo

    D. Nuno Gomes

3. Ronaldo made his senior Portugal debut against_____?

    A. Kazakhstan

    B. Brazil

    C. USA

    D. England

4. Ronaldo's first senior goal for Portugal was scored against _____?

    A. England

    B. Netherlands

    C. Spain

    D. Greece

5. How many direct goal involvements did Ronaldo have at Euro 2004?

    A. 0

    B. 4

    C. 1

    D. 2

6. Ronaldo's first ever World Cup goal was scored against_____?

    A. Germany

    B. France

    C. Iran

    D. England

7. Ronaldo captained Portugal for the first time in _____?

    A. 2007

    B. 2008

    C. 2006

    D. 2005

8. Ronaldo's only goal of the 2010 World Cup was scored against_____?

    A. Cote d'Ivoire

    B. North Korea

    C. Brazil

    D. Spain

9. How many matches has Ronaldo played at the FIFA World Cup?

    A. 15

    B. 10

    C. 30

    D. 22

10. Ronaldo's first ever international hattrick was against _____?

    A. Wales

    B. Republic of Ireland

    C. Northern Ireland

    D. Scotland

10 Trivia Answers

1. B – 34

2. C – Luis Figo

3. A – Kazakhstan

4. D – Greece

5. B – 4

6. C – Iran

7. A – 2007

8. B – North Korea

9. D – 22

10. C – Northern Ireland

Definitely the greatest Portuguese national team footballer of all time, Cristiano Ronaldo began representing the *Selecao* of Portugal in 2001 when he was selected for the Under-15 team. He also represented the under-17, under-20, under-21, and under-23 Portugal youth teams, with an overall record of 18 goals in 34 youth caps.

Ronaldo made his senior Portugal national team debut as a halftime substitute for Luis Figo, in a 1-0 victory over Kazakhstan in August 2003. He was subsequently named in Portugal's final squad for Euro 2004, held in his home country, and scored his first senior international goal in June 2004 in a 2-1 Euro 2004 group stage defeat to eventual tournament winners Greece. He also scored the opening goal of Portugal's 2-1 win over Netherlands in the semifinal and was named in the Team of the Tournament having scored two goals and provided two assists.

Ronaldo was Portugal's second highest goalscorer in their qualification campaign for the 2006 World Cup with seven strikes, and he duly opened his World Cup account with a well taken penalty in Portugal's second group game against Iran in June 2006, becoming his country's youngest ever scorer at the World Cup at 21 years and 132 days old.

Ronaldo captained Portugal for the first time on 6 February 2007, a day after he turned 22 and was given the Portugal number 7 jersey ahead of Euro 2008, after he had scored 8 goals in the qualifiers. During the tournament proper, he scored one goal and set up another in a thrilling 3-1 win over Czech Republic in the group stage, but Portugal's campaign ended abruptly with defeat against eventual runners-up, Germany, in the quarterfinals. Former Manchester United assistant manager Carlos Queiroz replaced Luiz Felipe Scolari as Portugal head coach following the country's dismal outing at Euro 20008, and Ronaldo was made permanent Portugal captain in July 2008.

Ronaldo did not score a single goal during Portugal's qualification campaign for the 2010 World Cup, and the country initially narrowly missed the tournament, eventually qualifying via a playoff victory over Bosnia & Herzegovina. Ronaldo scored his only goal of the 2010 World Cup in a 7-0 rout of North Korea, but was named Man of the Match in that game and the other two group games against Brazil and Cote d'Ivoire. Portugal's campaign ended in the Round of 16, after losing 1-0 to eventual winners Spain.

Ronaldo scored 7 goals, including two in the playoff tie against Bosnia and Herzegovina to help Portugal reach Euro 2012. Portugal were drawn in a tough group that included Denmark, Germany, and the Netherlands at the tournament. Ronaldo scored both goals in Portugal's 2-1 win in the final group game against the Netherlands and the only goal in their quarterfinal victory over Czech Republic, before the *Selecao* agonizingly crashed out on penalties following a goalless draw with eventual champions, Spain.

Ronaldo scored 8 goals in Portugal's 2014 World Cup qualifying campaign, and earned his 100th senior cap and first hattrick of his international career in two qualifying games against Northern Ireland. As Portugal did not qualify via the regular series, Ronaldo scored all four goals in a thrilling 4-2 aggregate win over Sweden in the playoffs. His hattrick in the second leg at Stockholm drew him level with Pauleta as Portugal's joint highest all-time top goalscorer, before Ronaldo's brace in a 5-1 friendly win over Cameroon in March earned him sole ownership of the record.

Despite being short of fitness going into the 2014 World Cup, Ronaldo played all 3 group games, setting up a late equalizer in the second group game against the USA, and scoring a late winner in the final group game against Ghana. Portugal crashed out at the group stage on goals difference, but Ronaldo's strike against Ghana, which was his 50th international goal made him the first Portuguese player to score at three World Cup tournaments.

Portugal's Euro 2016 qualifying campaign saw Ronaldo score five times and become the highest goalscorer in European Championships history (including qualifiers). At the tournament proper, Portugal drew all three group games and only made the knockout round as one of four best third-placed teams. Ronaldo became Portugal's most capped player in the second group game against Austria, and the player with most European Championships appearances and first to score at four Euro tournaments in an absorbing 3-3 draw in the final group game against Hungary.

Ronaldo's parried shot was converted by Ricardo Quaresma to ease Portugal past Croatia in the Round of 16, and Ronaldo scored Portugal's first spot kick in the shootout victory over Poland in the quarterfinals. Ronaldo drew level with Michel Platin as joint highest goalscorer at the European Championships, as his ninth goal in the competition set Portugal on their way to a 2-0 semifinal victory over Wales. Ronaldo was forced off 25 minutes into the showpiece against hosts France, bur Portugal eventually found a winner in the second half of extra time through substitute

Eder. Ronaldo lifted his and Portugal's first major trophy at a major international tournament, was named in the Euro Team of the Tournament for a third time and awarded the Silver Boot as joint second highest goalscorer with 3 goals and 3 assists.

Ronaldo was named as Man of the Match in all three group games for Portugal at the 2017 Confederations Cup, as he netted the winner in a 1-0 defeat of hosts Russia, and a penalty in a 4-0 win over New Zealand. He was allowed to miss the 2-1 third-place playoff win over Mexico after Portugal's 3-0 defeat on penalties to Chile in the semifinals.

Ronaldo scored 15 goals in Portugal's qualification matches for the 2018 World Cup and became the oldest player to score at hattrick at the FIFA World Cup in a thrilling 3-3 draw against Spain in Portugal's first match at the tournament. Ronaldo scored the only goal of Portugal's second group game against Morocco to overtake Ferenc Puskas as the highest European goalscorer of all-time. Ronaldo missed a penalty in the final group game against Iran that ended 1-1, before Portugal crashed out of the tournament following a 2-1 loss to Uruguay. Ronaldo's exploits at the tournament however, earned him a place in the FIFA World Cup Dream Team

Ronaldo missed the preliminary stage of the 2018/19 UEFA Nations League, but featured for Portugal in the finals as his hattrick against Switzerland fired his side to the final, which Portugal won 1-0 against the Netherlands. Ronaldo scored the 99th goal of his international career in Portugal's 2-0 win over Luxembourg in November 2020, a victory that guaranteed qualification for Euro 2020. His 100th and 101st goals were scored in a 2-0 win at Sweden in September 2020, making him the second male footballer to reach 100 international goals, and the first from Europe.

Ronaldo pulled clear of Michel Platini to become the outright most prolific player in Euros history with a brace in Portugal's 3-0 win over Hungary at Euro 2020. He netted another brace in Portugal's final 2-2 draw with France in the final group game to match Ali Daei's record of 109 international goals. Portugal bowed out of the tournament after losing 1-0 to Belgium in the Round of 16, but Ronaldo won the Golden Boot with 5 goals and 1 assist.

Ronaldo scored a pair of headed goals against Republic Ireland in a 2022 World Cup qualifier on 1 September 2021 to become the most prolific player in men's international football. He became the first male footballer to score at 5 different World Cups after converting a penalty against Ghana in Portugal's opening group game of the 2022 World Cup. Ronaldo was omitted from the starting lineup for Portugal's Round of 16 game against Switzerland, and his replacement, Goncalo Ramos scored a hattrick to help Portugal to a 6-1 win. Ronaldo's introduction as a second half substitute in Portugal's 1-0 loss to Morocco in the quarterfinal drew him level with Kuwait's Bader Al-Mutawa on 196 caps as the joint-most capped male footballer of all-time.

CRYPTOGRAM #1

Each letter in the phrase has been replaced with a random letter or number.

Try to decode the message.

A	B	C	D	E	F	G	H	I	J	K	L	M	N	O	P	Q	R	S	T	U	V	W	X	Y	Z
				5													10	23							

```
       R  7      E          E        R  E                      R
    ─── ───   ─── ─── ─── ─── ─── ─── ─── ─── ─── ───   ─── ─── ─── ─── ─── ───
     7  10    11  5   7   6  25   5       6  10   5   6  12    25   6   9  10  26   9
            E     E                    S         E   R  S          R
    ─── ─── ─── ─── ─── ─── ─── ─── ─── ─── ─── ─── ─── ─── ─── ─── ─── ───
    12   5   3   5   8   9   6   8   9   23  20  24   5  10  23  17   6  10
```

PROFILE AND STYLE OF PLAY

"Ronaldo can score with either of his feet, his head and now he is scoring with the goal at his back. I bet he can score on a wheelchair."

- Ryan Giggs

10 Trivia Questions

1. At Sporting Lisbon, Ronaldo was deployed as a _____?

   A. Centre forward

   B. Right winger

   C. Left winger

   D. Attacking midfielder

2. Ronaldo's signature moves do not include_____?

   A. Dribbling

   B. Step-overs

   C. Flip-flap

   D. Long throws

3. How many goals has Ronaldo scored using his head?

   A. 112

   B. 70

   C. 90

   D. 82

4. Which of Ronaldo's attributes caught the eye of his manager at Sporting?

   A. Dribbling

   B. Shooting

   C. Tackling

   D. Heading

5. How tall is Cristiano Ronaldo?

    A. 180 cm

    B. 183 cm

    C. 187 cm

    D. 193 cm

6. Ronaldo scored the first freekick of his career against _____?

    A. Wigan

    B. Millwall

    C. Reading

    D. Portsmouth

7. The knuckleball technique used by Ronaldo in striking freekicks is also common to _____?

    A. Roberto Carlos

    B. David Beckham

    C. Juninho Pernumbucano

    D. Zinedine Zidane

8. In what area of the pitch has Ronaldo been mostly deployed in the latter stages of his career?

    A. Left wing

    B. Centre forward

    C. Right wing

    D. Attacking midfield

9. Ronaldo's main attacking partner in his first season at Juventus was

    A. Mario Mandzukic

    B. Federico Bernardeschi

    C. Moise Kean

    D. Juan Cuadrado

10. How many freekick goals has Ronaldo scored?

    A. 40

    B. 58

    C. 66

    D. 34

10 Trivia Answers

1. B – Right winger

2. D – Long throws

3. A – 112

4. A – Dribbling

5. C – 187 cm

6. D – Portsmouth

7. C – Juninho Pernumbucano

8. B – Centre forward

9. A – Mario Mandzukic

10. B – 58

Cristiano Ronaldo has been a versatile forward from the outset, capable of playing on either flank or as a centre forward, and despite being predominantly right-footed, he is quite good with both feet. He has constantly evolved tactically to suit his strengths or meet the demands of his coaches.

At the start of his career, he was mostly deployed as a right winger as he used his pace, agility, and dribbling skills to get past opponents and deliver crosses into the penalty box during his time with Sporting Lisbon. He was well known for flair and dribbling, mostly exhibiting an array of feints and tricks such as step-overs, chops, and the flip-flap which became his signature moves.

As he matured, Ronaldo tremendously transformed his physique, developing a well-built body that enabled him keep possession of the ball under pressure, and well-built leg muscles that enhanced his aerial capabilities. His brute strength and jumping ability, coupled with his elevation, heading accuracy, and towering frame of 187 cm put him at an advantage in winning aerial duels. These characteristics make him a good candidate as a target-man and lethal poacher, resulting in many headed goals.

Combined with his heightened work rate and stamina, his goalscoring improved significantly, as he was given leeway to drift from the leftwing to central areas where he could finish off attacking moves. He also added creativity to his game, dropping into midfield to pickup the ball and utilizing his vision and passing attributes in creating chances for his teammates.

Ronaldo took on more central and attacking roles in his final seasons during his first stint at Manchester United, playing as striker, supporting striker, or attacking midfielder at times. He developed into a proficient goalscorer, capable of finishing from close range or from distance thanks to his remarkable ball-striking ability. He became a set-piece specialist, noted for his curling powerful freekicks that used the knuckleball technique pioneered by Juninho Pernumbucano. He also popularized a trademark posture where he stands with his legs wide apart and lets out a breath before striking the ball.

Ronaldo persisted in an offensive role at Real Madrid, while his creative and defensive inputs were significantly reduced. First deployed as a centre forward, he was eventually moved back to his preferred left wing, although in a flexible role that allowed him drift into central areas and finish off chances, or drag away defenders with his movement to open up spaces for his teammates. Real Madrid's counter-attacking pattern of play enhanced his consistency and efficiency, as evidenced by his remarkable record-breaking goalscoring exploits.

Ronaldo played in various offensive roles in his debut season at Juventus, depending on whom he was paired with. He was often deployed in a free role, either as a central striker or in his niche position on the left wing in a 4-3-3 or 4-2-3-1 setup, interchanging positions with Croatian striker Mario Mandzukic.

Ronaldo was also allowed to drop deep or drift to the right wing to gain possession of the ball, playing a greater role in the build-up than during his final seasons at Real Madrid. He was also capable of opening up spaces for his teammates with smart runs and movement off the ball, or finishing off chances with his feet or head by getting onto the end of passes and crosses.

CRYPTOGRAM #2

Each letter in the phrase has been replaced with a random letter or number.

Try to decode the message.

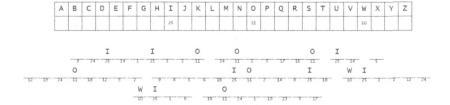

INDIVIDUAL ACCOLADES AND PERSONAL RECORDS

"I see myself as the best footballer in the world. If you don't believe you are the best, then you will never achieve all that you are capable of."

- Cristiano Ronaldo

10 Trivia Questions

1. Ronaldo won his first ever individual accolade in the year _____?

   A. 1991

   B. 1993

   C. 2008

   D. 2000

2. How many players had won all four main PFA and FWA awards in a single season before Ronaldo?

   A. 5

   B. 2

   C. 10

   D. 0

3. Ronaldo became Portugal's all-time highest goalscorer in _____?

   A. 2014

   B. 2016

   C. 2018

   D. 2011

4. Ronaldo won his first Ballon d'Or when he was _____?

    A. 20 years old

    B. 22 years old

    C. 23 years old

    D. 26 years old

5. Ronaldo became Portugal's most capped player in _____?

    A. 2012

    B. 2016

    C. 2021

    D. 2020

6. Ronaldo became the oldest player to score a World Cup hattrick at the age of_____?

    A. 33

    B. 35

    C. 37

    D. 31

7. Ronaldo has scored in how many consecutive international tournaments?

    A. 11

    B. 12

    C. 13

    D. 14

8. Ronaldo's record for most goals at the European Championships currently stands at _____?

    A. 15

    B. 14

    C. 13

    D. 12

9. Apart from Cristiano Ronaldo, how many other players have scored at 5 World Cups?

   A. 4

   B. 2

   C. 1

   D. 0

10. Ronaldo became the most prolific player in men's international football after he scored against_____?

    A. Scotland

    B. Republic of Ireland

    C. Sweden

    D. Northern Ireland

10 Trivia Answers

1. B – 1993

2. D – 0

3. A – 2014

4. C – 23 years old

5. B – 2016

6. A – 33

7. C – 13

8. B – 14

9. D – 0

10. B – Republic of Ireland

Cristiano Ronaldo's glittering career has seen him pick up numerous individual accolades as well as set and break abundant records. He picked up his first individual accolade, the Best Player award, at the Adelino Rodrigues children's tournament when he was only eight years old.

The iconic forward has won the coveted Ballon d'Or five times, and FIFA's award for Player of the Year three times. He has also been named FPF Portuguese Player of the Year on five occasions. Ronaldo was the first player to scoop all four main awards handed out by the Professional Footballers Association (PFA) and Football Writers Association (FWA) in the same season, doing so in 2006/07 and 2007/08. He was also been named Premier League Player of the Season (2006/07, 2007/08), La Liga Best Player (2013//14), and Serie A Footballer of the Year (2019/20).

Ronaldo has won the European Golden Shoe four times and is the only player to finish as top goalscorer in the English, Spanish and Italian leagues, picking up a Premier League Golden Boot (2007/08), three *Pichichi* Trophies (2010/11, 2013/14, 2014/15), and a *Capocannonerie* (2020/21).

Ronaldo is not left behind in terms of individual records as he has the most goals and joint-most caps in men's international football. He is also the first and only male footballer to score a goal at both 5 World Cups and 5 European Championships and he has made more appearances at the Euros than any other player.

Ronaldo also scored the most goals in a single UEFA Champions League season (17), most UEFA Champions League goals overall (140), most goals in the knockout rounds of the UEFA Champions League (67), most goals in a single UEFA Champions League group stage (11), joint-most UEFA Champions League hattricks (8), most successive seasons as UEFA Champions League top goalscorer (6), most top goalscorer awards in the UEFA Champions League (7) and a whole host of other accolades and records too numerous to mention.

Word Scramble #2

1. ACINISOTR _____
2. EYNTAPL _____
3. REFE IKCK _____
4. HTA KIRCT _____
5. VSJUUTEN _____
6. SPTINGRO PC _____
7. LA RNSSA _____
8. NTACEMESRH UEDITN _____
9. AELR RDMDAI _____
10. LUGPAORT _____
11. LINITAA SIERE A _____
12. AL IALG _____
13. IREEMPR EUGEAL _____
14. REAIMDA _____
15. GTHRI FOETOD _____
16. OGAT _____
17. DLO FDRATROF _____
18. GONISAAT BRUEBANE _____
19. DRE DILEV _____
20. AALILZN TMSADIU _____

PERSONAL LIFE & PHILANTHROPY

"At the moment, there is no better player than Cristiano. He was one of those who looked out for me at first, he's a really nice guy."

- Toni Kroos

10 Trivia Questions

1. Ronaldo's father died as a result of a_____?

   A. Car accident

   B. Heart attack

   C. Liver condition

   D. Cancer

2. Ronaldo split from Russian model Irina Shayk in _____?

   A. 2010

   B. 2011

   C. 2015

   D. 2017

3. Ronaldo's first child was born in which country?

   A. England

   B. Spain

   C. Italy

   D. USA

4. Ronaldo had a daughter with Georgina Rodriguez in _____?

   A. 2012

   B. 2017

   C. 2014

   D. 2019

5. Ronaldo won a libel suit against which of these tabloids?

   A. The Daily Mirror

   B. The Daily Mail

   C. The Manchester Daily

   D. The Daily Times

6. Currently (February 2023), how many children does Ronaldo have?

   A. 2

   B. 3

   C. 4

   D. 5

7. Ronaldo donated the damages from his 2008 libel suit against the Daily Mirror to _____?

   A. Church

   B. Charity

   C. A Football academy

   D. Trade Union

8. Ronaldo became a Global Artist Ambassador for Save the Children in _____?

   A. 2011

   B. 2012

   C. 2013

   D. 2014

9. Following the 2004 Indian Ocean earthquake & tsunami, Ronaldo paid a visit to_____?

   A. India

   B. Indonesia

   C. Pakistan

   D. Thailand

10. In 2015, Ronaldo was hailed as the most charitable sportsperson in the world after he made a donation worth_____?

    A.   3m pounds

    B.   5m pounds

    C.   7m pounds

    D.   10m pounds

10 Trivia Answers

1. C – Liver condition

2. C – 2015

3. D – USA

4. B – 2017

5. A – Daily Mirror

6. D – 5

7. B – Charity

8. C – 2013

9. B – Indonesia

10. B – 5m pounds

Ronaldo's father, Jose, died in September 2005 as a result of liver complications due to alcoholism when Ronaldo was only 20 years old. He retains a harmonious relationship with his mother and three siblings, with whom he is seen at most of his award presentations.

Cristiano Ronaldo is father to five children. His first son was born on 17 June 2010 in the United States of America. He retains full custody of the child and according to an agreement with the mother, her identity has never been publicly disclosed. Ronaldo also had a 5-year relationship with Russian model Irina Shayk, which ended in January 2015.

On 8 June 2017, Ronaldo confirmed that he had become a father to twins born in the USA through surrogacy. He is presently in a relationship with Argentine-born Spanish model Georgina Rodriguez, with whom he had a daughter in November 2017. The couple expected another pair of twins in 2022, but only the female twin survived as the male twin died during childbirth.

Ronaldo has publicly stated that he does not drink alcohol, and won a libel suit against British tabloid *Daily Mirror*, for their article that reported Ronaldo having too much alcohol at a nightclub while recuperating from an injury in July 2008. He also has no tattoos of any kind as he frequently donates blood voluntarily.

Ronaldo recently moved with his family to the Kingdom of Saudi Arabia, following his move to Saudi Premier League side, Al Nassr, at the end of 2022. He has been allowed to stay with his partner, although laws of the Kingdom prohibit couples living together before marriage.

Ronaldo has contributed to several charitable efforts throughout his long and prosperous career. He visited Aceh, Indonesia, in the aftermath of the 2004 Indian Ocean earthquake and Tsunami in a bid to raise funds for reconstruction and rehabilitation. The damages he received from the libel suit against *Daily Mirror* were donated to a charity in his native Madeira. He donated 10,000 pounds to the Madeira hospital that saved his mother's life during her struggle with cancer, and pledged to participate in a charity match to be played in Madeira between FC Porto and players from Madeiran-based clubs Maritimo and Nacional, in support of the victims of the flood that devastated Madeira in 2010.

Ronaldo and his then agent, Jorge Mendes, paid for specialist treatment for a 9-year-old kid from the Canary Islands suffering from terminal cancer, and in

December 2012, Ronaldo liaised with FIFA's "11 for Health" programme to spread awareness amongst children on how to avoid vices such as drug addiction, and prevent HIV, malaria, and obesity.

Ronaldo became Save the Children's new Global Artist Ambassador in January 2013, an effort to help in the fight against child hunger and obesity, and in March 2013, he consented to be the ambassador for Mangrove Care Forum in Indonesia, an organization striving to spread awareness about mangrove conservation.

After donating 5 million pounds towards relief efforts for a 2015 earthquake that killed over 8,000 people in Nepal, Ronaldo was named as the world's most charitable sportsperson, and in June 2016, he donated the whole of 600,000 euros bonus he got from Real Madrid's 2015/16 UEFA Champions League triumph. Ronaldo has recently launched CR7Selfie, a charitable selfie app for Save the Children that lets donors take a selfie with him in various poses and outfits.

His relationship with former Manchester United manager, Sir Alex Ferguson, has been one of the highest points of his career. Sir Alex exerted a father figure role on his life and watched him grow during a difficult moment. There are reports that Sir Alex even sold then star striker, Ruud van Nistelrooy because he was bullying young Cristiano. Even in the latter years of his career, Ronaldo has been quick to give a lot of credit and reverence to the man who signed him as a boy and guided him to become a man.

Crossword #3

ACROSS

(2) Birth City

(4) Italian League Name

(5) Birth Country

(8) English Club he played for

(9) Spanish Club he played for

(10) Italian Club he played for

DOWN

(1) Saudi Arabian Club he played for

(3) Birth Month

(6) English League Name

(7) Porteguese Club he played for

PUZZLE SOLUTIONS

House of Ballers

Across

[2] Birth month
[5] Most played team
[7] Team after Portugal
[9] Balon D' Or wins
[10] #1 sport in England

Down

[1] CR7's nationality
[3] Birth city
[4] First team
[6] Name in the USA
[8] First trophy for Portugal

Ronaldo

Solution

Unscramble these words to solve the puzzle!

1. NAICSTOIR ROAOLND __CRISTIANO RONALDO__

2. SSNHPIA AL GLIA __SPANISH LA LIGA__

3. OATG __GOAT__

4. HTE BETS __THE BEST__

5. FIAF LRDWO PCU __FIFA WORLD CUP__

6. ITLAINA IEERS A __ITALIAN SERIE A__

7. LTPRUOAG __PORTUGAL__

8. MNHOCSPAI GLEUAE __CHAMPIONS LEAGUE__

9. AGLENDN ERMPEIRE LEGEUA __ENGLAND PREMIERE LEAGUE__

10. OUREENPA PAONIHHPCMIS __EUROPEAN CHAMPIONSHIP__

11. TCNHRSAEEM UDIETN __MANCHESTER UNITED__

12. EARL DRIMDA __REAL MADRID__

13. TNEUSVUJ __JUVENTUS__

14. TPO REOCSR __TOP SCORER__

15. NAPSI __SPAIN__

16. CRKTTHAI __HATTRICK__

17. DLENGO OBTO __GOLDEN BOOT__

18. OLANB RDO __BALON DOR__

19. EKRISRT __STRIKER__

20. CLGAOO __GOLACO__

Ronaldo

```
P  S  L  E  N  H  N  Y  W  L  X  I  S  Q  K
O  R  X  A  X  X  T  L  O  E  L  R  E  B  Q
R  V  L  U  I  P  C  I  R  R  C  K  R  S  Y
T  S  G  F  J  S  H  I  L  O  X  V  I  A  K
U  E  N  G  L  A  N  D  D  N  C  G  E  X  P
G  N  C  E  H  Y  B  F  C  A  H  O  A  T  M
A  D  A  B  H  Q  Z  Z  U  L  A  A  Q  H  B
L  P  B  H  E  H  F  A  P  D  M  T  B  E  A
K  E  U  R  O  S  I  Z  L  O  P  I  R  B  L
M  Y  I  U  N  K  F  B  V  W  I  K  G  E  L
M  W  Y  R  U  D  A  L  A  A  O  M  U  S  O
Y  L  A  L  I  G  A  O  H  R  N  J  X  T  N
X  V  U  G  F  V  W  O  C  P  S  C  W  S  D
S  K  Z  E  W  W  F  X  N  K  W  Y  U  Y  O
A  W  V  Q  D  I  A  L  A  Q  V  O  T  H  R
```

RONALDO	THEBEST	SERIEA	ENGLAND
LALIGA	WORLDCUP	PORTUGAL	BALLONDOR
GOAT	FIFA	CHAMPIONS	EUROS

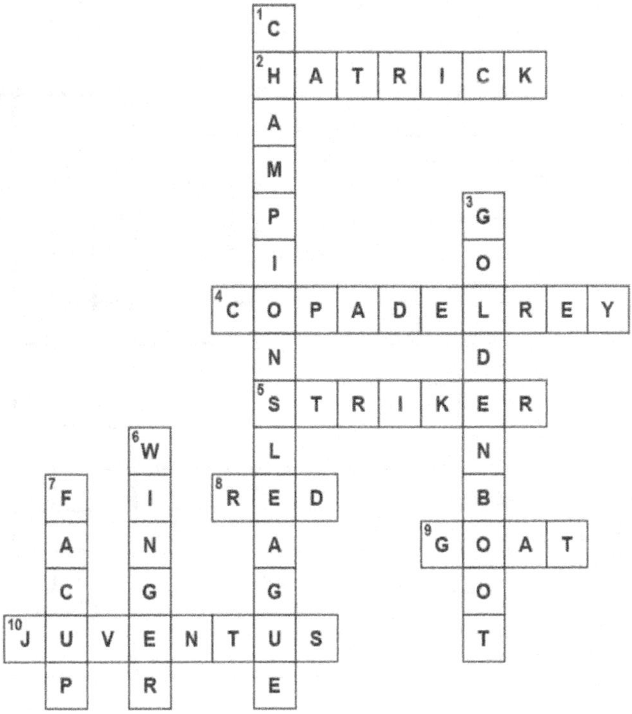
1 CHAMPIONS LEAGUE
2 HATRICK
3 GOLDEN BOOT
4 COPA DEL REY
5 STRIKER
6 WINGER
7 FA CUP
8 RED
9 GOAT
10 JUVENTUS

Across

[2] 3 goals

[4] Spanish Cup

[5] Position after 30

[8] Portugal team color

[9] Nickname

[10] Team in Italy

Down

[1] 5 Trophies

[3] Top scorer trophy

[6] Position before 30

[7] English Cup

Ronaldo

```
G T B O S Q S T C X X U O O D
A O X C M A N U N I T E D G B
S P J J M J U H A T T R I C K
U S Z R T U R D H K J R Q I W
G C L F Q V G E A C S Q S G X
O O N R I E Z R T D T L Q A Y
L R J E A N F B F H N T E K I
D E Y E A T N Y O Z B N K C T
E R L K Q U W P O A W F L C B
N S O I B S F B H E A D E R D
B I Y C R E A L M A D R I D C
O Z C K T S P A I N K O P K R
O O M Q T B Y V C B V E I Z D
T A J A T I X N I Y X T B H A
I A R H F F X V T H Q G N C G
```

MANUNITED	REALMADRID	FREEKICK	JUVENTUS
HEADER	TOPSCORER	SPAIN	HATTRICK
GOLDENBOOT	DERBY		

Solution

S	I	V	I	U	Z	Z	K	Y	I	G	Z	M	Y	N
K	N	W	C	Y	U	T	J	T	C	L	J	G	Q	C
I	S	S	E	W	D	K	D	K	O	Z	H	L	X	S
L	P	S	L	H	W	F	A	C	N	J	U	Z	H	B
L	I	X	E	Q	L	E	A	D	E	R	S	H	I	P
S	R	V	B	S	U	P	Q	N	T	M	M	A	S	V
U	A	J	R	P	A	T	H	L	E	T	E	M	G	D
L	T	G	I	E	A	U	T	L	R	M	M	B	I	E
W	I	S	T	E	T	P	O	W	E	R	R	I	V	D
D	O	E	Y	D	H	S	R	S	G	Q	C	T	T	A
U	N	Y	U	O	H	B	C	B	T	Q	M	I	R	Y
O	S	T	R	I	K	E	R	J	D	B	B	O	L	E
C	C	X	G	D	H	N	R	Y	L	P	C	N	M	R
V	D	E	D	I	C	A	T	I	O	N	H	O	Q	D
B	P	E	E	P	L	A	Y	E	R	S	B	K	J	O

PLAYER	AMBITION	STRIKER	SKILLS
SPEED	CELEBRITY	ATHLETE	INSPIRATION
POWER	DEDICATION	LEADERSHIP	ICON

A	B	C	D	E	F	G	H	I	J	K	L	M	N	O	P	Q	R	S	T	U	V	W	X	Y	Z
	11			5							12						10	23							

C R 7   B E C A M E   A   R E A L   M A D R I D

7 10   11 5 7 6 25 5   8   10 5 6 12   25 6 9 10 26 9

L E G E N D   A N D   S U P E R S T A R

12 5 3 5 8 9   6 8 9   23 20 24 5 10 23 17 6 10

Ronaldo

A	B	C	D	E	F	G	H	I	J	K	L	M	N	O	P	Q	R	S	T	U	V	W	X	Y	Z
								25						11								10			

```
 C   R   I   S   T   I   A   N   O     R   O   N   A   L   D   O     I   S     A
 9  24  25  14   1  25   5   2  11    24  11   2   5  17  15  11    25  14     5

 E   U   R   O   P   E   A   N     C   H   A   M   P   I   O   N   S   H   I   P     W   I   N   N   E   R
12  19  24  11  18  12   5   2     9   8   5   6  18  25  11   2  14   8  25  18    10  25   2   2  12  24

         W   I   T   H     P   O   R   T   U   G   A   L
        10  25   1   8    18  11  24   1  19  23   5  17
```

1. ACINISOTR   CRISTIANO

2. EYNTAPL   PENALTY

3. REFE IKCK   FREE KICK

4. HTA KIRCT   HAT TRICK

5. VSJUUTEN   JUVENTUS

6. SPTINGRO PC   SPORTING CP

7. LA RNSSA   AL NASSR

8. NTACEMESRH UEDITN   MANCHESTER UNITED

9. AELR RDMDAI   REAL MADRID

10. LUGPAORT   PORTUGAL

11. LINITAA SIERE A   ITALIAN SERIE A

12. AL IALG   LA LIGA

13. IREEMPR EUGEAL   PREMIER LEAGUE

14. REAIMDA   MADEIRA

15. GTHRI FOETOD   RIGHT FOOTED

16. OGAT   GOAT

17. DLO FDRATROF   OLD TRAFFORD

18. GONISAAT BRUEBANE   SANTIAGO BERNABEU

19. DRE DILEV   RED DEVIL

20. AALILZN TMSADIU   ALLIANZ STADIUM

Ronaldo

Across

[2] Birth City
[3] Italian League Name
[4] Birth Country
[5] English Club he played for
[7] Spanish Club he played for
[8] Italian Club he played for

Down

[1] Saudi Arabian Club he played for
[2] Birth Month
[4] English League Name
[6] Portuguese Club he played for

With love, from The House of Ballers team…

Hello our fellow FootBaller.

We really hope you enjoyed RONALDO: The Complete Story of a Football Superstar.

From the bottom of our hearts, thank you for purchasing and reading it to the end.

We create these books to allow people to, not just expand their knowledge around their favorite clubs and players, but to keep the passion we all have for the game lit and alive.

Life can come with many challenges and setbacks. But something that never leaves our side is our love for the game.

If you enjoyed reading this book, we'd like to kindly ask for your feedback and thoughts in the review section on Amazon.

This would really help us to keep spreading the word and creating the highest quality books and content for football fans all across the globe.

>> Scan the QR Code above to leave a short review on Amazon <<

Thanks in advance!

Ball out,

The House of Ballers team.

Made in United States
North Haven, CT
26 October 2023

43129061R00070